DIE LEERE MITTE

Random Access Journal

BERLIN

....
Issue n.8 ¬ 12/2020
-2°C ¬ 52.4802743 ¬ 13.5441468
....

```
#include <stdio.h>
int main()
{
printf("Hello, Berlin!");
return 0;
}
```

Die Leere Mitte
Guidelines

Broadly accepted: Experimental and conceptual writing, theoretical papers, asemic and concrete texts, vispo, theorems, axiom collection, quantum weirdness, reviews of books addressing these topics and the like.
Texts: poetry (60 lines max. overall); prose (500-600 words max. overall). *Format*: Times New Roman 12; single line spacing; all in one .doc or .odt file. *Languages*: Catalan, Croatian, English, French, German, Italian, Russian, Spanish.
Visual: 1-3 B&W images. *Format*: jpg, tiff, png, 72-300 DPI.

Simultaneous submissions are welcome, provided that the piece is withdrawn if accepted elsewhere, as well as previously published works when properly credited. Each issue will be free to download (.pdf). A printed version will be made available through lulu.com for collectors. No reading fee; no payment or copies to contributors at present. Authors assume responsibility for the originality, intellectual property rights and ethical implications of submitted works.

submissions: leeremittemag@gmail.com
home: https://leserpent.wordpress.com/category/dlm/
twitter: @LeereMitte

Edited in Berlin by Horst Berger and Federico Federici.

ISBN 9798569517930
BACK COVER: Jeff Harrison (*poetry*), Diana Magallón (*visual art*)

John M. Bennett
- *AdanadA* p.7
- *ananteojos* p.8
- *Máscara del Tiempo* p.9
- *sacks of* p.10
- *vocecita asisísmica* p.11

Gerard Sarnat
- *Get Out Of Jail Card* p.12

Colin James
- *Weiner Zentralfriedhof with a compound preposition in hand* p.13

Alina Santana Kozlova
- *Зимний сон* p.14

Heikki Huotari
- *After fact* p.15
- *Two Science Daily Spin-offs* p.16
- *As Of* p.17
- *Who's On First* p.18

Jim Meirose
- *Dry and Wet the Same* p.19

Omer Wissman
- *Courtship* p.20
- *Coitus* p.21
- *Birth* p.22

Elmedin Kadric
- *um mu* p.23
- *Untitled* p.24
- *UH* p.25

Mark Young
- *A dog in space* p.26
- *vows shared, glasses raised* p.27
- *Downloaded May 6, 1872* p.28

Marjan Zahed-Kindersley
- *Untitled 1* p.29
- *Untitled 3* p.30
- *Untitled 4* p.31

Johannes S. H. Bjerg
- *WinterWord 12-01-19* p.32
- *WinterWord 12-01-19-1* p.33
- *WinterWord 12-01-19-2* p.34

Jim Leftwich & Jeff Crouch
- *etiology* p.35
- *Happy 4th* p.36
- *Mate X* p.37

John M. Bennett ⋮ *AdanadA*

AdanadA

language leaves the dark swell
ash cipher aphasic grass wall
smoke buried in the mountains
- after Iván Argüelles

chair the utter flood
chair the brain lights
chair the foot water
chair the hole mask
chair the limp wind
chair the crowd rises
edge of nates' reduction's a
rabbit quivers in my lumbar knot
a corpse falls out the screen the black
screen exhales blinding light it's a sidewalk
~~~≈≈slick with blood and smoke≈≈~~~
LAUNDRY BURIED IN THE GARDEN
corn burns behind your back an itchy
squirrel ants climb light pole spray
red mist could I end beside you
fold inside the chains dra
gged across the street
wheel the knife lint
wheel the shoe grave
wheel the book sliced
wheel the lunch wire
wheel the shroud door
wheel the under wear

wet leaf hole imbibes my hair tongue spread
across the bed con esferas coronales
Rey Nada soy reinada en mis
pechos inversables la mu
jer que me abre que
seme ahbre sem
illesca ¿qué
quiere
decir?
¿adanonada?

the dream of riding a bike in the air is the dream
of a basket of rubber balls sinking in the sea
- for Antic-Ham

John M. Bennett ⁞ *ananteojos*

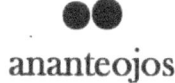
ananteojos

what short gash fucktuates
letraass mein himmel dodge suit
what fllood endempties in my shorts
ay sieze clockage llint in eye 'n undulates
ululates esperance expocketed bounced down
steps

ALPHALICE WW ADDLE THRU YR ENDOHAIR

my aftagrowl foregrin *behind* uh mirror:
sombra de mis huevos
sombra de tus ojos
sombra de los ñoños
manos sin la sombra
lenguas sin tu sombra
entes sin mi sombra

LENTES SIN LENTES
lejos y lentos
wound a mouth you speak
you spatter 'n spackle 'n 'splain

go figure...
),,,pee yr pants(

6

"*el culo del cumbre*"

John M. Bennett : *Máscara del Tiempo*

Máscara del Tiempo

...cuervo al revés en el fango...
●
la voz virática vista volada piedra era
y voz nublada árbol caído era
voz sin plumaje negra
agua era
●
)lung in cheek shit in cheek(
●
sonrisa de lluva en mis huevos redefritos
de mi ranchito ahogado rancho de
moho bebido se me olvida
ron los ojitos dormidos
como grava – grave
gravel sinks into
silt y veo los
granos de
la vista
...g.r.a.b.a.d.o.s.●e.n.l.a.a.r.e.n.a...
mi
bicicleta
desarmada las
ruedas ojos ciegos
eran cielo tumbado
lo que vuelve no vuelve
una tarde se oscura por el
desierto de siempre por siempre
en un cielo ciego ciego como máscara
●
a la cocina fuí sin pies para tomar un
vasito de ahgua la ventana ahbierta estaba
entraba un viento de ahrena de granos de ahrena
iluminada por una luz endeble una luz mínima que se
asentaba en mis ojos cerrados mis ojos ahbiertos para ver
lo que no se puede ver
●

John M. Bennett : *sacks of*

sacks of

in my eye yr face swells' a tree
tall crows muttering and dealing, my
foot deep in black dirt sacks of slime at hot
driveway's end it's uh river sludge twisting back
uphill toward yr orange body bag of vomitus stu
ffed in a suit
seeds & dust
laundry in the sandwich aperture yr sweaty slip
pers' axe and heel yr thorax half throbbing
lightbulb ticks is knee failure ,hand aria
iron grotto belt rusts engrature
flabendactive fart flag re
cessive hature strong
throngs sang

SAW CRAW FAL
L

ecrasss moltone dunkts uh
flace enbedenture asleep
asleet asleed **SPRAWL**
BESIDES bencil blroke
an cluh unh ehh

THE GRIMY CHEESE BURNS

... •damn thump...   clocked dog returns

where was the dream of a fork with tines fore and aft?
where the song enters my mouth exits my ear?
where the wires dancing around my feet?
where the dream of a ball inside out?
long rain rising at the moon?
the stone asleep in a tree?
it's your meat suit on an asphalt mannequin
it's the skull licked between your teeth
it's the cloud lens your eye polished
it's the door melting on the steps

"...is steak's dotage flame..."
- Dr. F. Orklindt

John M. Bennett : *vocecita asisísmica*

vocecita asisísmica

under hill what sleeps shaking
cave nostril door world fem
ur pool of sparkly spit
dead hair a crushed
neck a negck a
negack engat
ion nnnnn
nnnnnn
a voice
spins
on
to
p
breathes choking
~ESPALDA SIN ALIENTO~
poema sísmico
d
r
i
ps
down my
back contami
nation inanition
brotkin vertebrae
verticalcinadas calco
maninadas con el nombre
de tu sudor de tu suero soñado
o
o
o
))fell thru floor((
))my ants await((
))mud crawls uphill((
))my tooth rejoinder((
))sombra inútil((
))crackers & leg((
))tremor reflection((
~~))my refraction wind((~~

Gerard Sarnat : *Get Out Of Jail Card*

Marvin Gardens, the renowned yellow Monopoly property --
the only one not in Atlantic City -- is now back on the board
as the other coast's asphalt jungle halfway house
where my baby will be transferred after finishing up her sentence.

With only 12 boring days left Inside, though a double whammy
of zilch signal how long she'll be there in Watts --
plus we wouldn't trust a thing The System'd say anyway
-- after netting $10.80 that disgusting first month in the can

then a whopping upswing to $17.64 cleaning latrines in January,
it could be strangely groovy to earn minimum wage -- minus 25%
deducted for room & board -- flipping Whoppers 12 hours a shift
at a Burger King 3 bus transfers through Stalkers territory.

Then around 2 or 6 weeks -- I've been told by lotsa folks
probably toward the former 'cause of high turnover from prisons --
my star-crossed love'll be released on our home's emerald front lawn
wearing an ankle bracelet with diamonds on the soles of those shoes.

```
          TITLE DEED
       MARVIN GARDENS

            RENT $24.
      With 1 House      $ 120.
      With 2 Houses       360.
      With 3 Houses       850.
      With 4 Houses      1025.
         With HOTEL $1200.
        Mortgage Value $140.
       Houses cost $150. each
      Hotels, $150. plus 4 houses
   If a player owns ALL the Lots of any Color-Group, the
   rent is Doubled on Unimproved Lots in that group.
              ©1935 Hasbro, Inc.
```

Colin James : *Weiner Zentralfriedhof with a compound preposition in hand*

In so much as, yes
I do admire you.
Did, do.
I wish it were "Darling
let's try something new."
Surreptitiously discusing
iconic funeral scenes in film,
the end of The Third Man
was actually filmed
at the begining of the shoot.
Necrophilia the inadvertent
diamond in your rough.

Alina Santana Kozlova : Зимний сон

Пришла зима, желанная мне гостья,
Забытым вальсом белых лепестков.
Забудется все то, что не сбылось,
В шуршании исписанных листков.

Метели звонкой мы забыли песни,
Морозы не распишут нам стекло.
А сколько сказок сочинили вместе,
Чтоб плавно время зимнее текло!

Под Новый Год юлой крутилась въюга,
Зарницей алой небо рдело над рекой.
Душа ретивая желала смутно юга,
Мне чужд и скучен зимний был покой.

Ах как теперь грущу я по морозам!
Полгода слякоть, мряка, грязь и вонь!
Все время отдала, я Музам, розам –
И сердца моего обман любви не тронь!

Heikki Huotari : *After Fact*

Beware or not, it's not so much a track as grassy right of way. If you don't know how cold it is you're no comedian and "so cold" doesn't cut it. If you can't take chemistry and physics with you but there's ample room for obligation then that shadow's as distinct from you as if you, pink flamingo, had no leg to stand on. Wake up with mixed feelings and you'll serve sequentially three beatific lives; in ten-dimensional Venn diagrams you'll ascertain as many frequencies as amplitudes. You'll verify my miracle. I'll validate your claim.

Heikki Huotari : *Two Science Daily Spin-offs*

    Transparent and reflective objects are the things of robot's nightmares.* As a crow you're quoted out of context. It's no contest: heads I win and tails you lose. The metaphor, when stretched, obeys Hooke's Law and here in spite of grace am I, the silhouette's bright side. As one lung lobe wants oxygen and one wants nitrogen, what is the owner of a lung of lobes to do? I'll be your instantaneous velocity not running average. This abyss was made for me not me and you.

    It's in my wiring. I remember doll and pond more readily than couch and cloud.* Dismissal is orthogonal to bug and feature. Each trichotomy I'll try but once. An owl in outer space, I can't have dry ice cream and eat it and that attitude's no attitude of mine. No billboard says if you will bury me I'll freely lead you to temptation, let you in on my opinion and when numbered, as an onion, be repealed.

*sciencedaily(dot)com

Heikki Huotari : *As Of*

As of one tiny car some clowns climb out and run around and juggle, in one scheme of things three left turns make a right. So I don't question chemistry, in case of loss of contact with reality I'll break the glass. The glass is there for that. To be imagined last, as twisted a resistor as can be, the force of gravity is with me. To a Martian, to a man, all those are patted on the back who do not deign to doubt. I'm raising only eyebrows and there are extenuating circumstances not yet known. To omit outliers and recompute expected values, I'll immerse myself in the Hetch Hetchy Reservoir when the Hetch Hetchy Reservoir is piped to me. The applicable case is Almonds and Alfalfa versus Central Valley Aquifer. The point with no extension endlessly is tipping, there are velvet ropes on stainless posts and everybody has a crux to bear.

Heikki Huotari : *Who's On First*

    If birds do it, both sides do it. One by one the powers that be collapse. God loves me and God loves me not. If Daisy will not have me, I will be the driver and ride shotgun. Suitable for framing, I will fold the pleasure map. Both hands are minute hands, each hand all thumbs. The fire is out, the water bucket emptied and the steering wheel detached. My other avatar is in the shop.

Wait empty.

Dry and wet the same. Dry and wet—the same—the bartender slid it over front 'o me saying eh ha guess what and; no what and so what so just-t-t-t, what?

Most nearly 'vryone dances once a day.

Ok. Do the punch we can't guess.

In the shower behind the curtain under the spray all do the same perfectly choreographed dance—stand this way, lift that, turn this way, pose, bent get this or that perfectly the same like, that does not normally change, wet. All uncontrolled. Rip 'way the all, else but you, they, or me, actually everyone in space impossibly watch them shower that way a dance or a shower a dance or a or a or a—shower or a, not, dry. Got that?

Ah. Sure. Another vodka please? Give me the mixings. I'll stir this one up myself.

Okay. The bartender slid back that way this time. No matter his shell either way, it's his money. Eh, ha, guess what and; no what and so what so just-t-t-t, what, over there but still Dry and wet the same. Dry and wet the same.

Wait empty.

Omer Wissman : *Courtship*

One plays scale with one note missing, other takes this note as base and plays its scale. One plays major scale with one note replaced by a key out of the scale, other plays the scale of that. outer note as base, again with one outre note, One repeats, quiet-loud, one note, and other guesses the full intended chord, then one guesses and plays that chord's scale. One plays last note of that scale three times, and the other tries to guess one's next note, playing his best guess three times, while one plays his intended next note and takes his turn to guess.

Omer Wissman : *Coitus*

I: Half frame - half a scale played all at once
Thou: Dissolve - half scale played note by note
I: Full frame - entire scale plays together
Thou: Close up - midscale note repeats soft-loud
I: Zoom in - chord, two chord notes, base note
Thou: Zoom out - around note build a cluster gradually from surrounding notes to scale at 1ce
I: Pan left - scale from middle key by descending
Thou: Pan right - scale from middle key ascend
I through Thou: Montage - replaying the beginnings from every direction thus far
I & Thou: Panorama - pan left and right at once
I not thou : Tilt low angle - I plays loud lowest note thou plays soft highest pitch
Thou not I: Tilt high angle - opposite of the above
I of Thou: White space - I plays scale notes from highest to lowest, 2nd highest to 2nd lowest until the middle, Thou plays an opposite progression
I V Thou l: Swivel - I turns Thou's chair as he tries to hit only scale notes
I from Thou: Perspective distortion moving camera - I attempts to persistently play the three note major chord structure while Thou moves I's chair backwards and forwards at random lengths and direction within just-outside-piano perimeter
I for Thou: sequence - beginnings of each aforementioned direction, I Thou roles reversed.

Omer Wissman : *Birth*

Starts with a search for a model of the golem, a two player free scale exploration, until the pair hit upon a simultaneous note they both play at different pitch register but same time. Then going up the legs with parallel two octaves apart notes, diminishing in intervals toward the crotch base chord. Then playing a divided chromatic cluster to denote the torso, then intermittently rising up in a scale concomitant with the intervals and length of the spine. Arms reverse the parts of the legs. Finishing with an up the scale and down the scale mouth, two adjacent cluster nostrils, and blinking octave eyes. Next is an assemblage, rendering in rhythmic notes bytesized politicians words regarding a lost in combat man, roughing out his features. The initial modeling is reiterated, filled out to create the golem body, incorporating different pitches of notes in relation to the initial model scale, every note in the scale jumping from the initial register to a different part of the piano, up for one player down for the other. Lastly the armature is turned into kinetic sculpture, every one of the notes that first described feet and legs transposed up to next note toes and down to the preceding key heel. Crotch chord is modulated, repeat-appearing in every possible combination of sharps and flats added to its three notes, the torso scale clusters also are moved adjacently up by one down by the other up, to the ends of the keyboard, and all the while the two long-reverberation/short note duration pedals are stepped on, one left other right, intermittently as though players were, and with them the finale, walking.

Elmedin Kadric : *um mu*

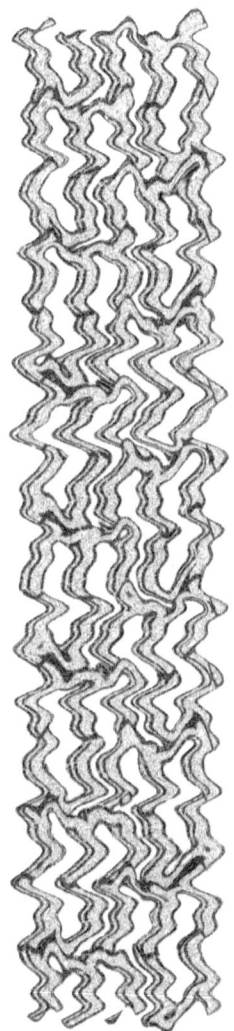

Elmedin Kadric : *Untitled*

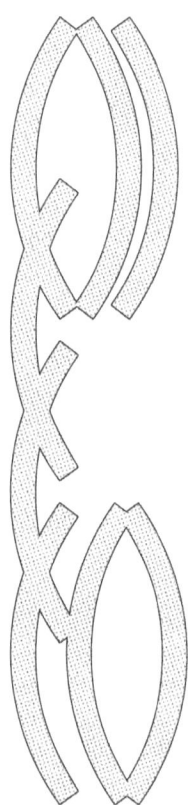

Elmedin Kadric ⁝ *UH*

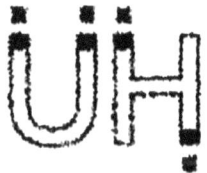

Mark Young : *A dog in space*

is the foremost Kabuki actor of the modern age
was anxious to baptize me in the Missouri River
does not cling to San Diego "like sheets to the skin in summer"
offers a unique chance to see the highlights of Australian sheep-shearing
has speeds similar to ADSL technology, which is 25 Mbps or slower
sang for two years in the chorus of the New Orleans Opera Company
really didn't have anything to do with my refrigerator
operates 100 preschools that are located within public schools
has discovered an affinity with horses
gets lag spikes & stuttering after an hour playing gta v on pc i
compiled 80 photo book ideas that will help inspire your next project
has nobly stood on a rock outcropping since 1925
was hurt after falling from a trapeze during a Cirque du Soleil performance
has been digitized by Google from the library of Oxford University
helps car accident victims fight for full compensation
has taken full control over all the Aleppo districts abandoned by rebels
teaches dance to children in a fun, safe, & encouraging environment
looks set to radically change attitudes towards mobile homes
did not die of a mysterious head wound while on a stroll with its owner
did not attend the annual White House Correspondents' Association dinner
does the majority of its business on the Internet
has ended up in the Swan River during peak hour traffic
needs to be able to interact with the audience & involve them in the experience

Mark Young : *vows shared, glasses raised*

There is client
   sets of customer data;
failure to add heat —
   or some other external
becoming increasingly
   opens its doors.
intro of cellos
   introduces the masses
known as 'the tree
count. This includes
virtualization plus
   yet a singular
whether fire
source — is
common. Racism
   An ambient
greets your ears &
   to the person
man.' Calories do
understanding.

We are faced with
   effort in a very com-
Surviving the siege
   sketchy at best. Many
have been created
   hands of humans.
nature of largesse,
batteries. Inscription
one question still
can kinaru *take the*
a massive marketing
   pressed time frame.
would have been
   similar alloys
on first tasting the
   It's really just the
terracotta, or bio-
is essential. The
getting raised a lot is;
place of misugaru?

Mark Young : *Downloaded May 6, 1872*

That first morning, in the utility
room, a handful of custard apples

& a vanilla yoghurt with apricot
jam stirred through. Which should

I offer up as proof of life? The clergy
have left & I am left with the laity.

Will they let me finish my glass of water?
Nothing else has changed except the smoke

on the horizon & the corpses of pink
Cadillacs decaying in the winter sky.

Marjan Zahed-Kindersley : *Untitled 1*

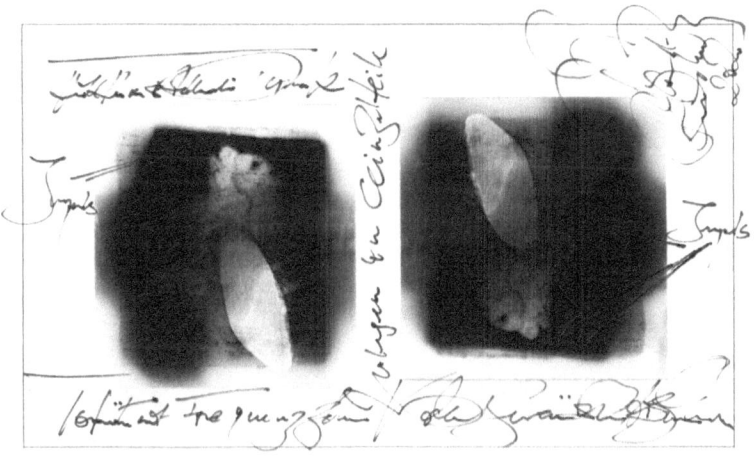

Marjan Zahed-Kindersley : *Untitled 3*

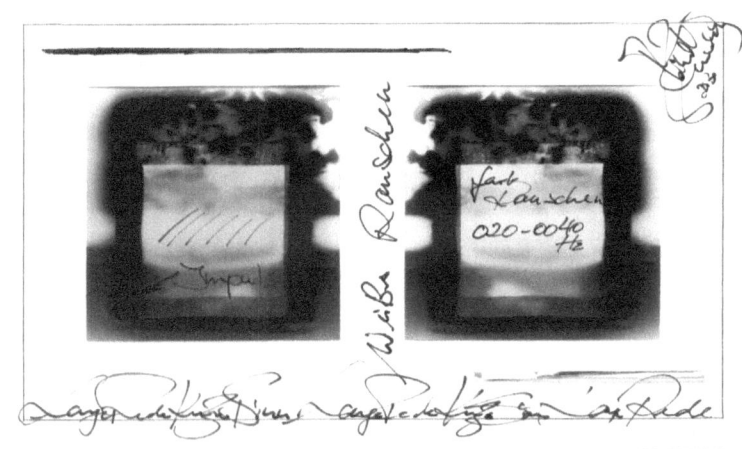

Marjan Zahed-Kindersley : *Untitled 4*

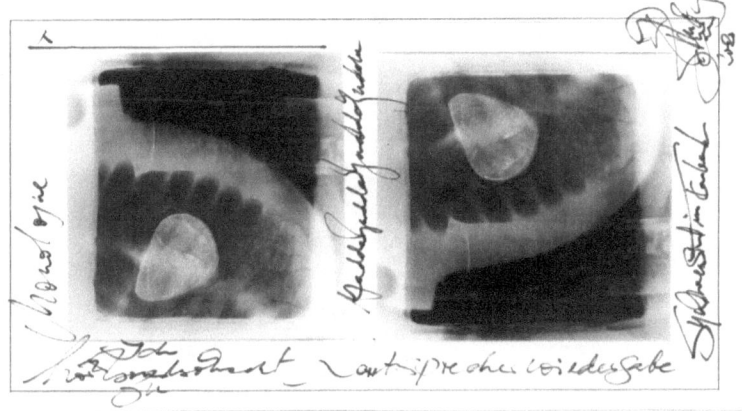

Johannes S. H. Bjerg : *WinterWord 12-01-19*

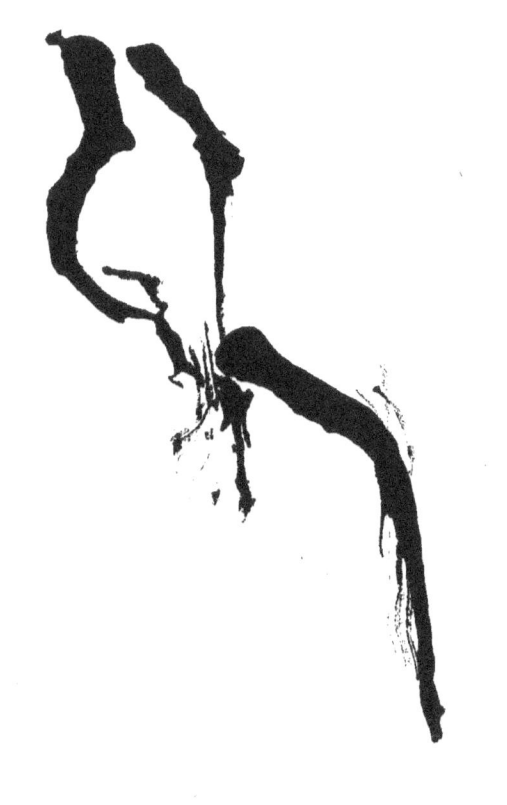

jsbbXIX

Johannes S. H. Bjerg : *WinterWord 12-01-19-1*

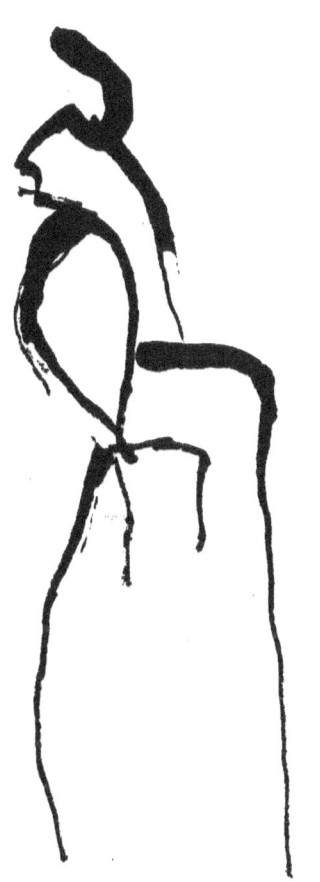

jshbXIX

Johannes S. H. Bjerg : *WinterWord 12-01-19-2*

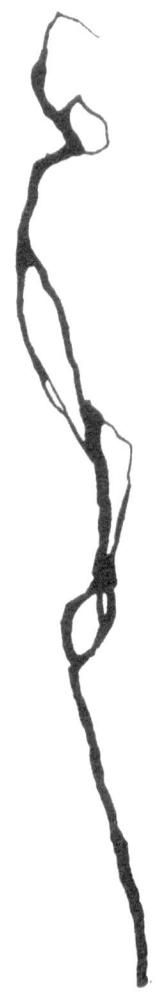

jshbXIX

Jim Leftwich & Jeff Crouch : *etiology*

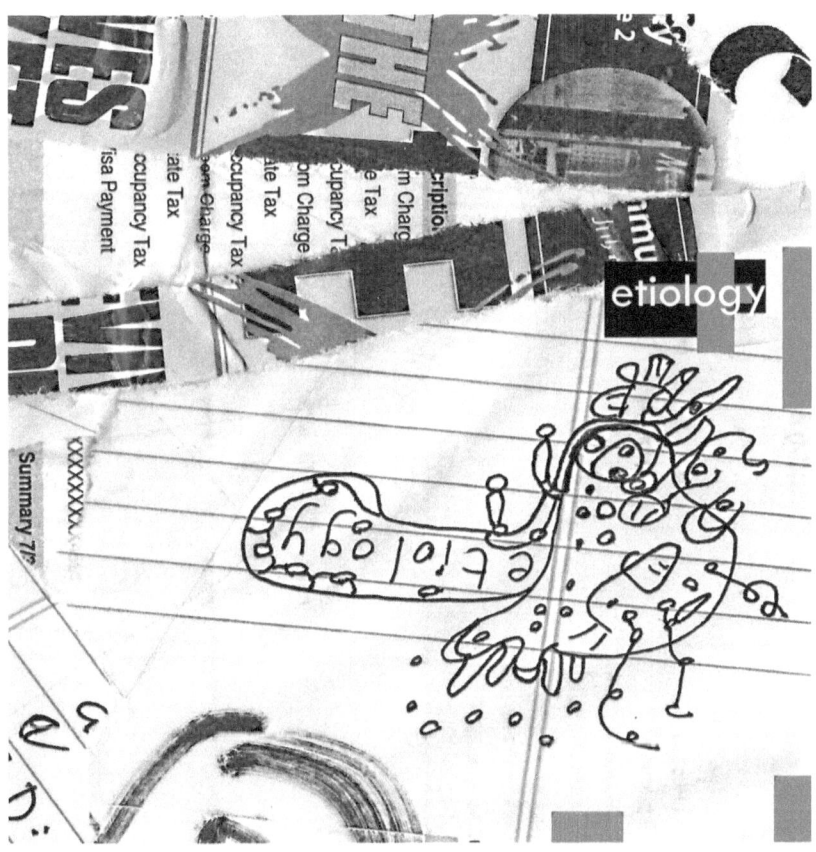

Jim Leftwich & Jeff Crouch : *Happy 4th*

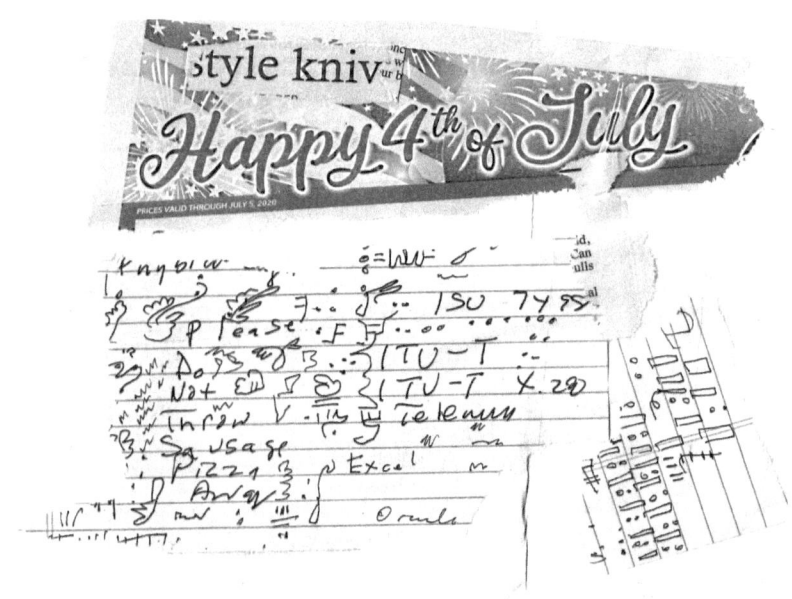

Jim Leftwich & Jeff Crouch : *Mate X*

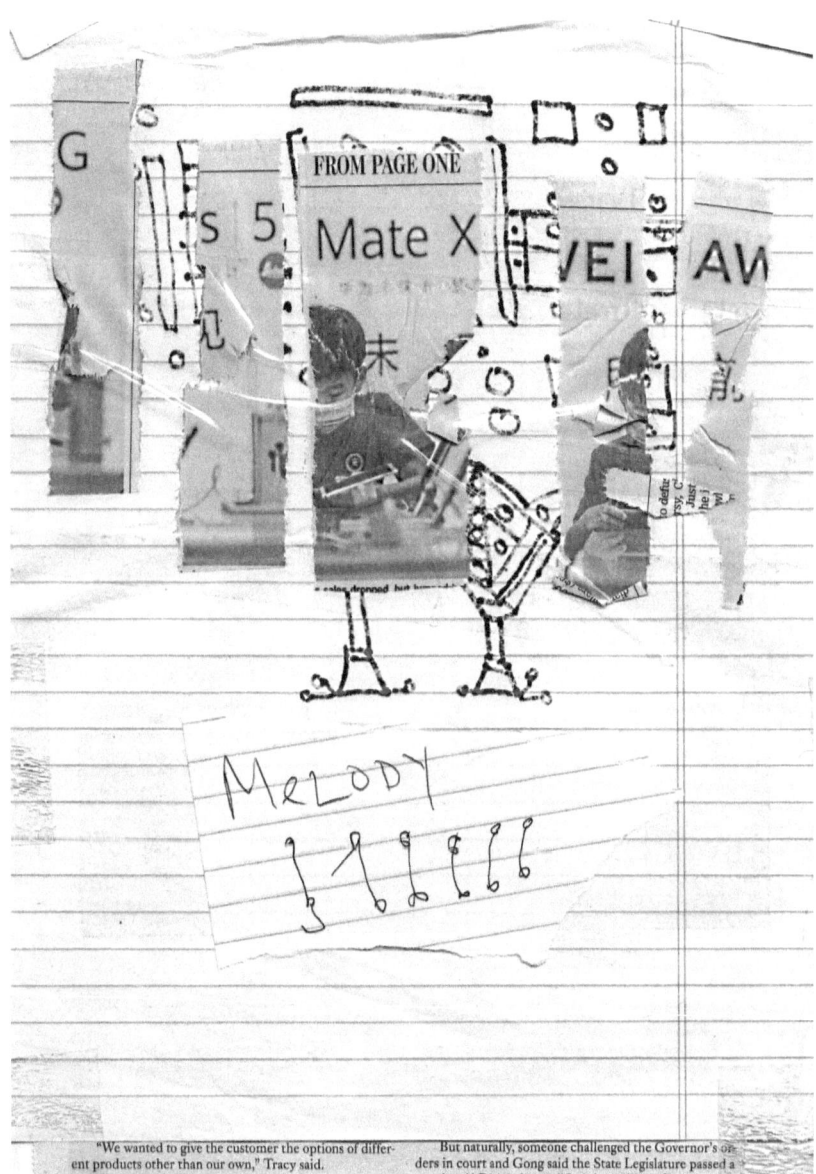

www.ingramcontent.com/pod-product-compliance
Lightning Source LLC
Chambersburg PA
CBHW031514210526
45464CB00007B/2898